Tidal Flow Dynamics and Background Fluorescence of the Atlantic Intracoastal Waterway in the Vicinity of Sullivan's Island and the Isle of Palms, South Carolina, 2011–12

By Paul A. Conrads, Celeste A. Journey, Jimmy M. Clark, and Victor A. Levesque

Prepared in cooperation with the
South Carolina Department of Health and Environmental Control

Open-File Report 2013–1077

U.S. Department of the Interior
U.S. Geological Survey

U.S. Department of the Interior
SALLY JEWELL, Secretary

U.S. Geological Survey
Suzette M. Kimball, Acting Director

U.S. Geological Survey, Reston, Virginia: 2013

For more information on the USGS—the Federal source for science about the Earth, its natural and living resources, natural hazards, and the environment, visit http://www.usgs.gov or call 1–888–ASK–USGS.

For an overview of USGS information products, including maps, imagery, and publications,
visit http://www.usgs.gov/pubprod

To order this and other USGS information products, visit http://store.usgs.gov

Contents

Figures

Tables

Conversion Factors, Datum, and Abbreviations

Inch/Pound to SI

Multiply	By	To obtain
Length		
foot (ft)	0.3048	meter (m)
Flow velocity		
foot per second (ft/s)	0.3048	meter per second (m/s)
Flow rate		
cubic foot per second (ft³/s)	0.02832	cubic meter per second (m³/s)

Temperature in degrees Celsius (°C) may be converted to degrees Fahrenheit (°F) as follows:

°F=(1.8×°C)+32

Horizontal coordinate information is referenced to the North American Datum of 1983 (NAD 83).

Specific conductance is given in millisiemens per centimeter at 25 degrees Celsius (mS/cm at 25 °C).

Concentrations of chemical constituents in water are given either in milligrams per liter (mg/L) or micrograms per liter (µg/L).

Abbreviations

ADCP	acoustic Doppler current profiler
ADVM	acoustic Doppler velocity meter
BI	Breach Inlet (station)
CH	Customs House (station)
EDS	Extended Deployment System
EST	Eastern Standard Time
GIS	Geographic Information System
IDW	inverse distance weighted
IOP	Isle of Palms (station)
kHz	kilohertz
NPDES	National Pollutant Discharge Elimination System
R^2	coefficient of determination
SI	Sullivan's Island (station)
SL	side looker
USGS	U.S. Geological Survey

Tidal Flow Dynamics and Background Fluorescence of the Atlantic Intracoastal Waterway in the Vicinity of Sullivan's Island and the Isle of Palms, South Carolina, 2011–12

By Paul A. Conrads, Celeste A. Journey, Jimmy M. Clark, and Victor A. Levesque

Abstract

To effectively plan site-specific studies to understand the connection between wastewater effluent and shellfish beds, data are needed concerning flow dynamics and background fluorescence in the Atlantic Intracoastal Waterway near the effluent outfalls on Sullivan's Island and the Isle of Palms. Tidal flows were computed by the U.S. Geological Survey for three stations and longitudinal water-quality profiles were collected at high and low tide. Flows for the three U.S. Geological Survey stations, the Atlantic Intracoastal Waterway by the Isle of Palms Marina, the Atlantic Intracoastal Waterway by the Ben M. Sawyer Memorial Bridge at Sullivan's Island, and Breach Inlet, were computed for the 53-day period from December 4, 2011, to January 26, 2012. The largest flows occurred at Breach Inlet and ranged from -58,600 cubic feet per second (ft³/s) toward the Atlantic Intracoastal Waterway to 63,300 ft³/s toward the Atlantic Ocean. Of the two stations on the Atlantic Intracoastal Waterway, the Sullivan's Island station had the larger flows and ranged from -6,360 ft³/s to the southwest (toward Charleston Harbor) to 8,930 ft³/s to the northeast. Computed tidal flow at the Isle of Palms station ranged from -3,460 ft³/s toward the southwest to 6,410 ft³/s toward the northeast. The synoptic water-quality study showed that the stations were well mixed vertically and horizontally. All fluorescence measurements (recorded as rhodamine concentration) were below the accuracy of the sensor and the background fluorescence would not likely interfere with a dye-tracer study.

Introduction

Proposed changes in water-quality limits for fecal coliform may have potential effects on the open shellfish beds (those beds where harvesting is allowed) near the effluent outfalls of the Sullivan's Island and the Isle of Palms wastewater treatment plants (fig. 1). A number of alternative study approaches can be used to better understand the potential connections between wastewater effluent and the shellfish bed, including dye-tracer studies, sediment sampling for wastewater indicators, and thermal plume tracking. To effectively plan such studies, data are needed concerning the flow dynamics and background fluorescence of the Atlantic Intracoastal Waterway near the effluent outfalls on Sullivan's Island and the Isle of Palms in South Carolina. Tidal flow dynamics of the Atlantic Intracoastal Waterway, located on the landward side of the barrier islands along the South Carolina coast, are quite complex because of reversing tidal flows, interconnected tidal creeks, multiple connections between barrier islands and the Atlantic Ocean, wetting and drying of extensive tidal marshes, and semidiurnal tides with a 5- to 7-foot (ft) vertical range. Often, flows in these systems are characterized by large, bidirectional tidal excursions during the flood and ebb tides and by small residual (net) flows over the tidal cycle.

Dye fluorometry is an established method for tracing the movement of water in many hydrologic settings. When used as a tracer, the concentration of a dye is directly proportional to its fluorescence. Background fluorescence can interfere or enhance the fluorescence of the dye, thereby causing overestimation of the movement and dispersion of the dye (Hartel and others, 2007). Elevated background fluorescence can be caused by optical brighteners commonly found in the effluent of wastewater treatment plants and septic tanks. Optical brighteners have the ability to fluoresce and interfere with the measurement of rhodamine dye used as a hydrologic tracer. Other sources of background fluorescence include naturally occurring humic substances that produce the "blackwater" of coastal waters, synthetic organic compounds that can reach the water during rainfall runoff, and various byproducts from pulp and paper production (Hartel and others, 2007).

The U.S. Geological Survey (USGS), in cooperation with the South Carolina Department of Health and Environmental Control, initiated a data-collection effort in 2011 to measure the tidal flow dynamics and background fluorescence in the

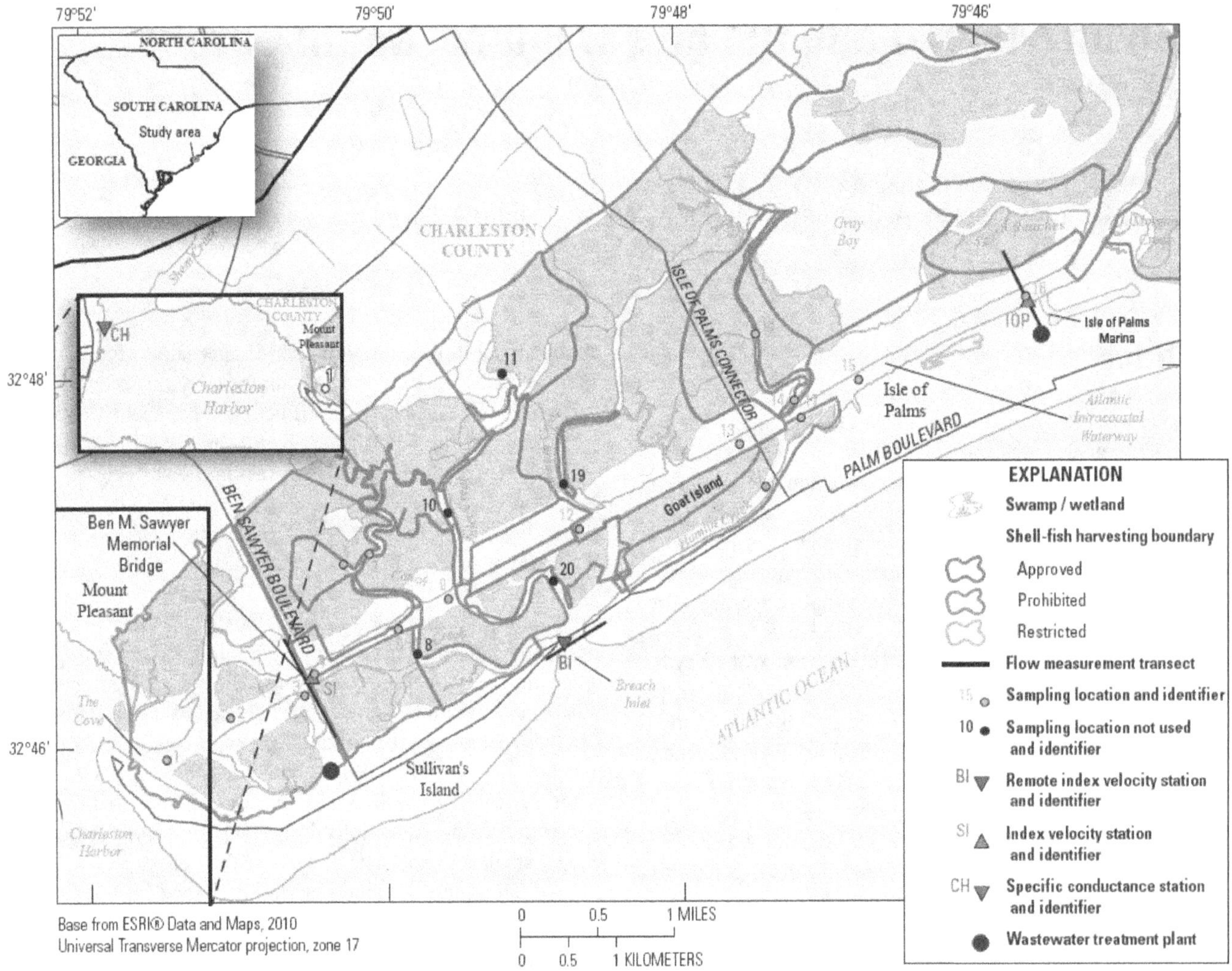

Figure 1.   Location of shellfish harvesting areas, index velocity stations, remote index velocity station, flow measurement transects, and water-quality sampling stations near Sullivan's Island and Isle of Palms, South Carolina. [BI, Breach Inlet station; CH, Charleston Harbor station; IOP, Isle of Palms station; SI, Sullivan's Island station]

Atlantic Intracoastal Waterway in the vicinity of Sullivan's Island and Isle of Palms. An important part of the USGS mission is to provide scientific information for the effective water-resources management of the Nation. To assess the quantity and quality of the Nation's surface water, the USGS collects hydrologic and water-quality data from rivers, lakes, and estuaries using standardized methods and maintains the data from these stations in a national database. This data collection effort will contribute to the understanding of complex flow and water-quality dynamics of near barrier islands along the South Atlantic coast.

The purpose of this report is to characterize tidal-flows and background fluorescence in the Atlantic Intracoastal Waterway in the vicinity of Sullivan's Island and Isle of Palms. The methods used to collect continuous velocity, stage, temperature and flow are described, as well as those used for discrete flow measurements. This report documents the development of three index velocity sites for the computation of continuous, including the development of stage curves, index-velocity ratings, and computation of continuous flow record. Water quality and background fluorescence are assessed using basic water chemistry data collected at profile stations.

Data Collection

To compute continuous tidal flows, two index-velocity stations were installed on the Atlantic Intracoastal Waterway at the Isle of Palms Marina and at the Ben M. Sawyer Memorial Bridge (referred to as the IOP station and SI station, respectively for this report; table 1 and fig. 1). Each station was equipped with an acoustic Doppler velocity meter (ADVM), water-level sensor, and temperature and specific conductance sensors. The ADVM, temperature, and conductance sensors for the IOP station were attached to a mooring piling at the southwestern end of the floating docks (fig. 2A). The

ADVM, temperature, and specific conductance sensors for the SI station were attached to the northeastern wooden fenders (fig. 2B). Stations were visited approximately every 3 weeks during the deployment to perform quality-assurance checks and to exchange batteries.

In addition to monitoring tidal velocity, gage height (also referred to as stage), and specific conductance, physical measurements of flow were made during approximately one-half of a tidal cycle at the index-velocity stations. These measurements were used to develop stage-area relations for the index-velocity stations and to develop index-velocity to mean-velocity relations for each measured cross section.

Breach Inlet (fig. 1) flow was measured and used as a remote index-velocity station to estimate the tidal flow exchange in the inlet between the Isle of Palms and Sullivan's Island. No monitoring instrumentation was installed at Breach Inlet (referred to as the BI station in this report, table 1), but physical measurements of flow were made for approximately one-quarter of a tidal cycle at the BI station. These measurements were used with the SI station stage data to develop a stage-area relation for the BI station, and the velocity data at the SI station were used to develop a relation between the SI index velocity and the mean velocity at the BI station. No time correction was applied to the SI station data used at the remote index-velocity site at the BI station.

To measure the background fluorescence of the Atlantic Intracoastal Waterway, a synoptic water-quality study was conducted on January 24, 2012. Prior to field data collection, 21 potential locations were identified for data collection and established in a Geographic Information System (GIS) point coverage. Of these 21 potential stations, 5 were omitted for logistical reasons (stations 8, 10, 11, 19, and 20) (fig. 1). Selected water-quality vertical profile locations included stations near the effluent-receiving creeks, tidal creeks, and within the main body of the Atlantic Intracoastal Waterway (fig. 1 and table 2). Depth profiles of background fluorescence,

Table 1. U.S. Geological Survey river monitoring stations near Isle of Palms and Sullivan's Island.

[USGS, U.S. Geological Survey; AIW, Atlantic Intracoastal Waterway; IOP, Isle of Palms; V, velocity; SC, specific conductance; GH, gage height; WT, water temperature; Q, flow; SI, Sullivan's Island; BI, Breach Inlet; CH, Customs House; S.C., South Carolina]

Station name	USGS station number	Acronym of station name used in this report	Physical properties	Period of record	Longitude (NAD 83)	Latitude (NAD 83)
AIW at Isle of Palms Marina at Isle of Palms, S.C.	324822079454000	IOP	V, SC, GH, WT, Q	December 2, 2011– January 28, 2012	-79°45'40"	32°48'22"
AIW at the Ben Sawyer Bridge at Sullivan's Island, S.C.	324623079503000	SI	V, SC, GH, WT, Q	December 2, 2011– February 7, 2012	-79°50'30"	32°46'23"
Breach Inlet at S.C. Highway 703 at Sullivan's Island, S.C.[1]	324634079484400	BI	Q	December 2, 2011– January 28, 2012	-79°48'44"	32°46'34"
Cooper River at Customs House at Charleston, S.C.	21720710	CH	SC	October 1, 1996– February 20, 2013	-79°55'26"	32°46'49"

[1]Remote index-velocity site and used the gage height and velocity data from the Sullivan's Island station.

Figure 2.   Views of the *A*, Isle of Palms, and *B*, Sullivan's Island monitoring stations on the Atlantic Intracoastal Waterway. Photographs by Victor Levesque, U.S. Geological Survey.

Table 2.   Water-quality station locations in the Atlantic Intracoastal Waterway near Sullivan's Island and Isle of Palms, South Carolina, on January 24, 2012.

[AIW, Atlantic Intracoastal Waterway; L, low tide; H, high tide; WWTP, wastewater treatment plant; S.C., South Carolina]

Station number[1] (fig. 1)	Station description	Location relative to AIW	Within shellfish harvesting areas	Cross-section profile	Tide
1	AIW in The Cove near Sullivan's Island	Main channel	No	No	L
2	AIW at mouth of The Cove nr Sullivan's Island	Main channel	No	No	H, L
3	Unamed cove off AIW at the WWTP outfall in Sullivan's Island	Cove	No	No	H, L
4	AIW at the east side of S.C. Highway 703 (Ben Sawyer) Bridge in Sullivan's Island	Main channel	No	No	H, L
5	AIW between the mouths of Narrows and Conch Creeks nr Sullivan's Island	Main channel	No	No	L
6	West fork of Conch Creek nr Sullivan's island within shellfish harvesting area	Tidal creek	Yes	No	H
7	East Fork of Conch Creek near Sullivan's Island within shellfish harvesting area	Tidal creek	Yes	No	H
9	AIW before the mouth of Inlet Creek near Sullivan's Island	Main channel	No	No	H
12	AIW before the mouth of Swinton Creek near Isle of Palms	Main channel	No	Yes	H, L
13	AIW at the Isle of Palms connector bridge at Isle of Palms	Main channel	No	No	H, L
14	Hamlin Creek near its mouth near Goat Island at Isle of Palms in shellfish harvesting areas	Tidal creek	Yes	Yes	H
15	AIW at Goat Island	Main channel	No	No	H
16	AIW at Isle of Palms Marina index-velocity station	Main channel	No	No	H, L
17	AIW at the Isle of Palms WWTP outfall east of Isle of Palms Connector Bridge	Main channel	No	Yes	H, L
18	Hamlin Creek north of AIW in Isle of Palms	Tidal creek	Yes	No	H
21	Hamlin Creek south of AIW in Isle of Palms	Tidal creek	Yes	No	H

[1]Five stations were omitted for logistical purposes (stations 8, 10, 11, 19, and 20).

dissolved oxygen, pH, specific conductance, and water temperature were measured at 14 stations during high tide (8:30 to 11:30 a.m. EST) and at 9 stations during low tide (13:00 to 14:30 p.m. EST). High-tide vertical profiles were measured at stations 2–4, 6, 7, 9, 12–18, and 21. Low-tide vertical profiles were created at stations 1–5, 12, 13, 16, and 17. At stations 12, 14, and 17 during high-tide conditions, cross-sectional profiles were measured at 25-percent, 50-percent, and 75-percent widths along the cross section to assess horizontal mixing. Where water depth made it feasible, measurements were made at 1-ft, 5-ft, 10-ft, and 15-ft depth intervals to assess vertical mixing.

Two YSI 6600-V2 Extended Deployment System (EDS) water-quality sondes were used in the data-collection effort. The primary sonde was equipped with dissolved oxygen, pH, specific conductance, water temperature, and rhodamine sensors. The rhodamine sensor was used to measure the background fluorescence; specifications for the water-quality sensors are listed in table 3. The secondary sonde was equipped with dissolved oxygen, pH, specific conductance, and water temperature probes and provided field verification of the primary sonde readings. Data from the secondary sonde are not presented in this report. On January 24, 2012, prior to field data collection, the sensors on both sondes were calibrated as described in the YSI User's Manual and the U.S. Geological Survey (USGS) National Field Manual (Wilde, variously dated; YSI Incorporated, 2011).

Continuous Velocity, Stage, Temperature, and Specific Conductance Data

The index-velocity stations were operated from December 2, 2011, to February 7, 2012. The two stations were instrumented with a SonTek Argonaut-SL (side-looker) ADVM equipped with a vertical acoustic beam for measuring water level (SonTek, 2009) and YSI 600R water-quality sampling sonde equipped with temperature and specific conductance sensors. At the IOP station, the ADVM, and temperature and

conductance sensors were mounted approximately 2 ft above the channel bottom. At the SI station, the ADVM, temperature, and specific conductance sensors were mounted about 6 ft above the channel bottom. The IOP station ADVM was configured to measure a horizontal distance range from 6.6 to 26.2 ft (2 to 8 meters) from the instrument. The SI station ADVM was configured to measure a horizontal range from 9.8 to 39.4 ft (3 to 12 meters) from the instrument. Both stations used a 240-second averaging interval at the start of each quarter hour (15-minute measurement interval). Because of the bidirectional flow paths at these stations, velocity and flow toward the northeast were defined as positive and velocity and flow toward the southwest were defined as negative. For the BI station, positive velocity and flow were toward the Atlantic Ocean, and negative velocity and flow were toward the Atlantic Intracoastal Waterway.

The time-series gage-height and index-velocity data for the IOP and SI stations indicate a typical semidiurnal tidal cycle of 2 low and 2 high tides per lunar day (fig. 3). Because of power supply problems, data ends for the IOP station on January 28, 2012. Data collection was discontinued for the SI station on February 7, 2012. The period of record for the BI station is identical to that of the SI station. The gage-height data are referenced to a relative datum for each station. During the data-collection period, the gage height ranged from 0.55 to 7.72 ft (7.17 ft total range) at the IOP station and ranged from 3.36 to 12.28 ft (8.92 ft total range) at the SI station. The velocity time-series data for the two stations are different in magnitude and primary direction. Maximum velocity ranged from -0.52 foot per second (ft/s) to the southwest (toward Charleston Harbor) and 0.91 ft/s to the northeast for the IOP station and ranged from -2.10 ft/s to the southwest to 1.91 ft/s to the northeast for the SI station.

The time-series of temperature and specific conductance data are shown in figure 4; temperature data ranges were almost identical for the IOP and SI stations, ranging from 7.4 to 17.4 °C at the IOP station and from 7.5 to 17.5 °C at the SI station. The specific conductance data for the two stations were similar in pattern, but differed in range. Specific

Table 3. Specifications for water-quality sensors on the YSI 6600 EDS-V2 sonde.

[C, degrees Celsius; mS/cm, millisiemens per centimeter; %, percent; ROX, rates of oxidation; mg/L milligrams per liter; μg/L, micrograms per liter; resolution, the smallest measurable increment; accuracy, the closeness of the measurement to the actual value]

Sensor	Sensor type	Range	Resolution	Accuracy
Temperature	YSI 6560	-5 to 50 °C	0.01 °C	+/- 0.15 °C
Specific conductance	YSI 6560	0 to 100 mS/cm	0.001 to 0.1 mS/cm	+/- 0.5% or 0.001 mS/cm
Optical dissolved oxygen	YSI ROX	0 to 50 mg/L	0.01 mg/L	+/- 1 % or 0.1 mg/L
pH	YSI 6561	0 to 14 units	0.01 units	+/- 0.2 units
Rhodamine fluorescence	YSI 6130	0 to 200 μg/L	0.1 μg/L	+/- 5% or 1 μg/L

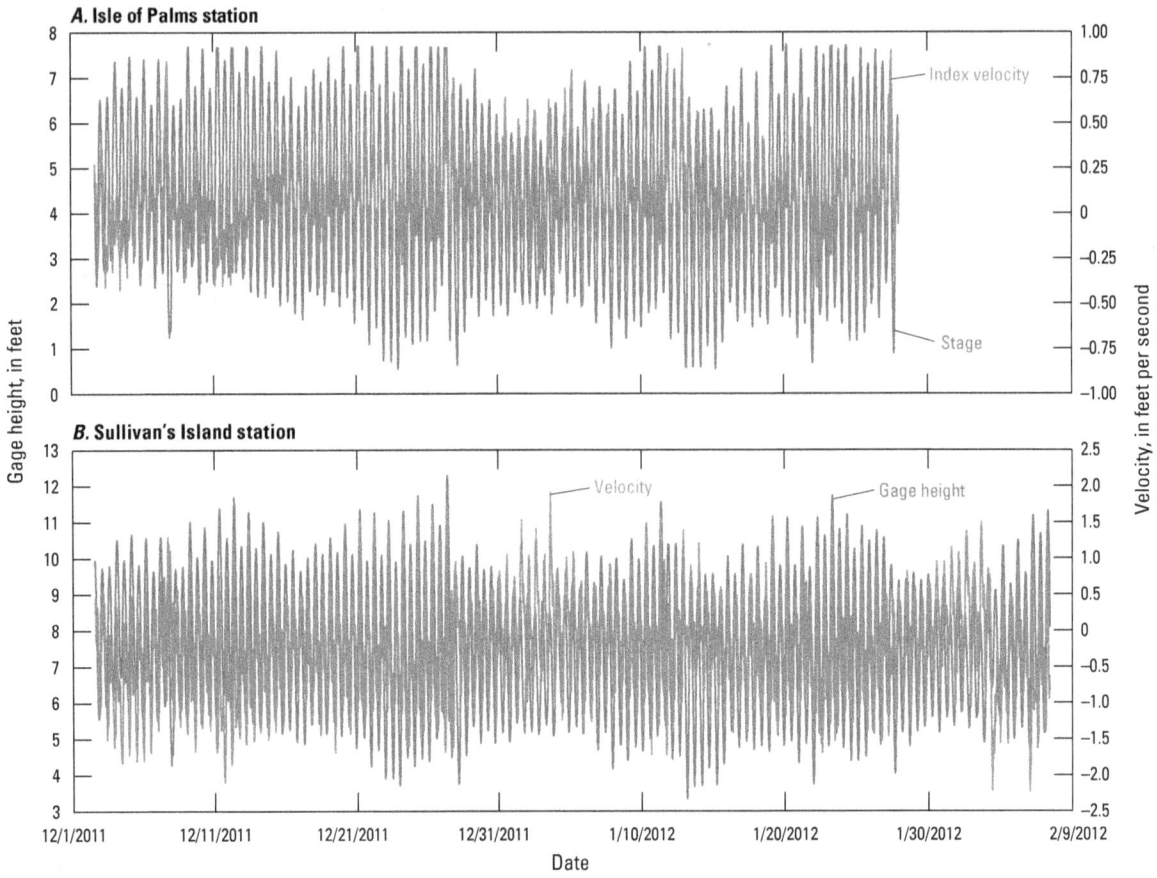

Figure 3. Gage height and index velocity data for *A*, the Isle of Palms station and *B*, the Sullivan's Island station.

conductance ranged from 49.3 to 53.6 millisiemens per centimeter (mS/cm) at the IOP station and ranged from 40.6 to 52.8 mS/cm at the SI station. The median specific conductance of 52.2 mS/cm for the IOP station was greater than the median value of 50.4 mS/cm for the SI station.

Discrete Flow Measurements

Once during the 60-day deployment, discrete tidal-cycle flow measurements were made over a 10- to 13-hour period in the Atlantic Intracoastal Waterway near the Isle of Palms Marina and at the Ben M. Sawyer Memorial Bridge. Additionally, discrete measurements were made over a 5- to 6-hour period at Breach Inlet. Measurements were made with Teledyne RD Instruments 1,200 kilohertz (kHz) Rio Grande acoustic Doppler current profilers (Teledyne RD Instruments, 2008) on January 23 and 24, 2012. Acoustic

flow measurement and processing procedures described by Mueller and Wagner (2009) were followed for the flow measurements.

The flow measured at the IOP station on January 23, 2012, ranged from –2,170 to 2,400 cubic feet per second (ft³/s), and flow at the SI station ranged from -4,630 to -107 ft³/s on January 23 and from -3,360 to 4,010 on January 24, 2012 (table 4). Although flow at the SI station did not reverse direction during the half tidal cycle on January 23, it was necessary to measure positive flows for a short period on January 24 in order to develop the index-to-mean velocity relation. The flow measured at the BI station on January 24 ranged from -3,470 to 35,960 ft³/s. The range of flow measured at the BI station is not representative of a typical tidal cycle. Data collection at the BI station was limited by the logistics of one field crew measuring flow at both the SI and BI stations and the priority of measuring positive flow at the SI station on January 24.

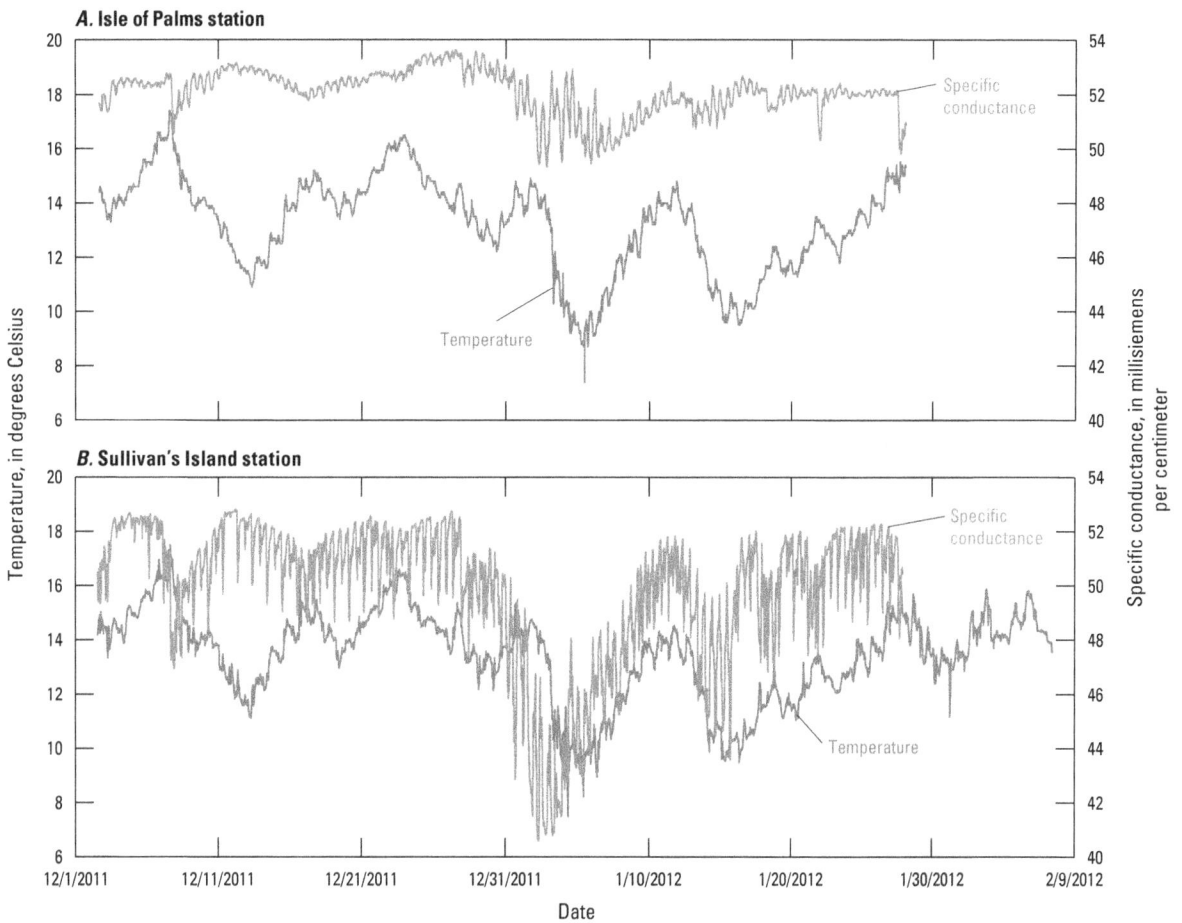

Figure 4.   Temperature and specific conductance data for *A*, the Isle of Palms station and *B*, the Sullivan's Island station.

Table 4.   Minimum and maximum flow measured during floodtide and ebbtide at the Isle of Palms, Sullivan's Island, and Breach Inlet stations.

[USGS, U.S. Geological Survey; Min, minimum; ft³/s, cubic foot per second; Max, maximum; AIW, Atlantic Intracoastal Waterway; S.C., South Carolina; na, data not available]

Station name	USGS station number	January 23, 2012		January 24, 2012	
		Min (ft³/s)	Max (ft³/s)	Min (ft³/s)	Max (ft³/s)
AIW at Isle of Palms Marina at Isle of Palms, S.C.[1]	324822079454000	-2,170	2,400	na	na
AIW at the Ben Sawyer Bridge at Sullivan's Island, S.C.[1]	324623079503000	-4,630	-107	-3,360	4,010
Breach Inlet at S.C. Highway 703 at Sullivan's Island, S.C.[2]	324634079484400	na	na	-3,470	35,960

[1]Postive flow is toward the northeast and negative flow is toward the southwest.

[2]Positive flow is toward the Atlantic Ocean and negative flow is toward the Atlantic Intracoastal Waterway.

Computation of Continuous Tidal Flow Data

The computation of continuous flow at the index-velocity stations was accomplished by following procedures described in Levesque and Oberg (2012). The first step was to develop stage-area ratings to establish the relation between tidal stage (gage height) at the station and cross-sectional area. The second step was to develop index-to-mean velocity ratings to convert the index velocity to a mean velocity for the cross section. The first two steps were accomplished by using the data from the tidal-cycle flow measurements. Flow was then computed by multiplying the cross-sectional area (computed using the stage-area rating) by the mean velocity (computed using the index-to-mean velocity rating).

Development of Stage-Area Curves

The cross-sectional areas measured during the tidal-cycle measurements were related to the measured gage height at the time of the measurements for the two index-velocity stations (fig. 5). Stage-area ratings that relate stage to cross-sectional area were developed using a selected acoustic Doppler current profiler (ADCP) transect and the USGS software AreaComp2-Version2 (*http://hydroacoustics.usgs.gov/indexvelocity/AreaComp.shtml*). AreaComp2 uses the stage and the projected area at the time of measurement and computes the cross-sectional area for any given stage. The BI station used the gage height data from the SI station because of the proximity of their locations.

Development of Index-Velocity Ratings

Side-looking ADVMs measure a horizontally oriented range-averaged velocity at a fixed elevation in the water column. The measured velocity typically is not the mean velocity for the cross section. In order to compute continuous flow at the index-velocity stations, the index velocity is calibrated to the measured-mean velocity of the cross section. Measured-mean velocities were computed from the tidal-cycle flow measurements made on January 23 and 24, 2012, by dividing the measured flow by the area determined from the stage-area rating. Simple-linear regression analysis was used to relate the index velocities to the measured mean velocities for the cross section for the three stations (fig. 6). Regression analysis for the IOP and SI stations indicated that the relation between the index velocity and the measured-mean velocity

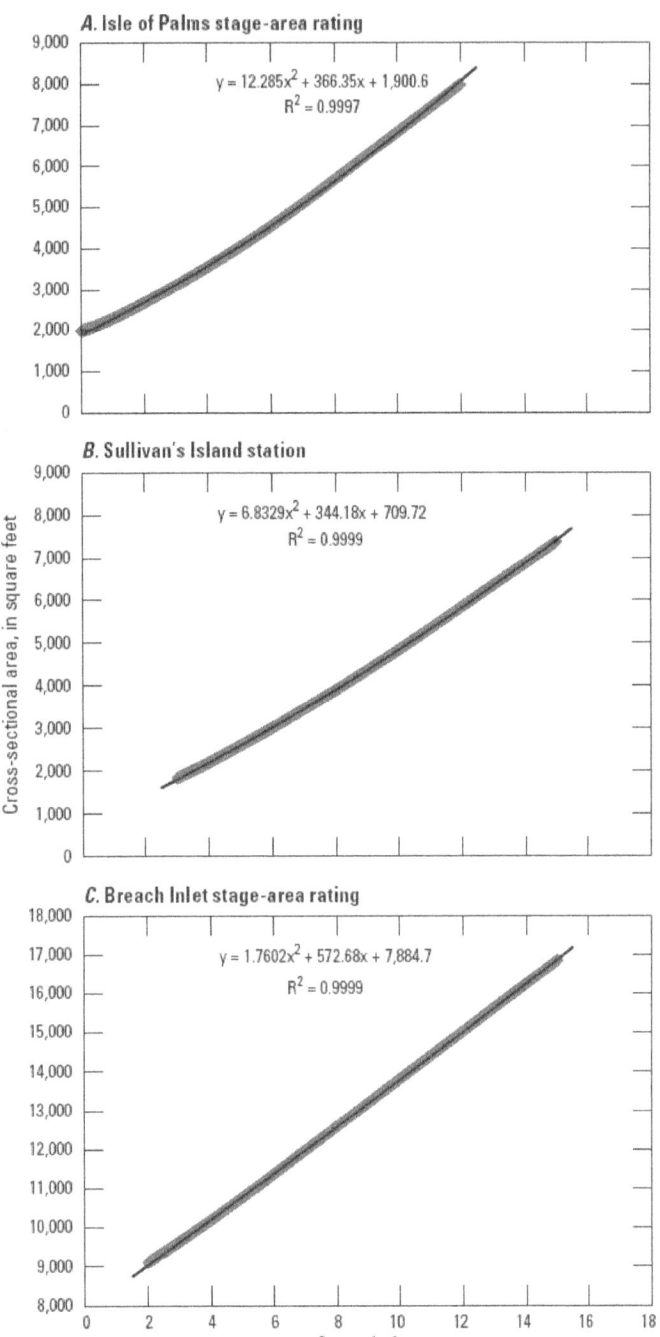

Figure 5. Stage-area ratings for the *A*, Isle of Palms station, *B*, the Sullivan's Island station, and *C*, the Breach Inlet station.

had changes in slope because of changes in flow direction. Residual plots of the simple-linear regression model were used to separate the data into two groups (positive and negative directions). Simple linear regression analysis was used on each data group to improve the accuracy of the index velocity rating at the IOP and SI stations. Because of limited flow data at the BI station, the data could not reliably be separated into positive and negative groups, so a simple-linear model was used for the BI index-to-mean velocity rating.

The velocity rating covers a range of mean velocity from –0.7 to 0.7 ft/s for the IOP station (fig. 6A) and –1.2 to 0.7 ft/s for the SI station (fig. 6B), and -0.3 to 2.7 ft/s for BI station (fig.6C). The standard error of the IOP station velocity ratings were 0.21 ft/s in the positive direction and 0.16 ft/s in the negative direction. The coefficients of determination (R^2) were 0.15 and 0.77 in the positive and negative direction, respectively. For the SI station velocity ratings, the standard error was 0.02 ft/s and 0.09 ft/s in the positive and negative direction, respectively, and the R^2s were 0.995 and 0.94 in the positive and negative direction, respectively. The BI station velocity rating standard error was 0.47 ft/s and a R^2 of 0.79.

The lower R^2 and higher standard error of the IOP station velocity rating, as compared to the SI station rating, is likely a result of complex flow patterns at the IOP ADVM location. The IOP station is located close to the confluence with Morgan Creek and the bend in the Atlantic Intracoastal Waterway to Seven Reaches (fig. 1). The flow patterns caused by the confluence of these flow paths contributed to the decreased accuracy of the IOP station velocity rating. The accuracy of the BI station velocity rating accuracy was adversely affected by limited number of available flow measurements and the use of data from of a remote ADVM that was not located in the Breach Inlet channel. Even with reduced accuracy, however, a reliable estimation of the continuous flow and residual flow direction is possible.

Continuous Tidal Flow Record

The continuous (15-minute interval) flow data at the index-velocity stations are a product of the mean velocity and cross-sectional area. The mean velocity is computed using the 15-minute index-velocity data and the index velocity rating, and the cross-sectional area was computed using the 15-minute stage data and the stage-area rating. The flows into the study reach of the Atlantic Intracoastal Waterway were different in magnitude and direction for each station (table 5 and fig. 7). The flow magnitude at BI station was substantially greater than the IOP or SI station flows and ranged from

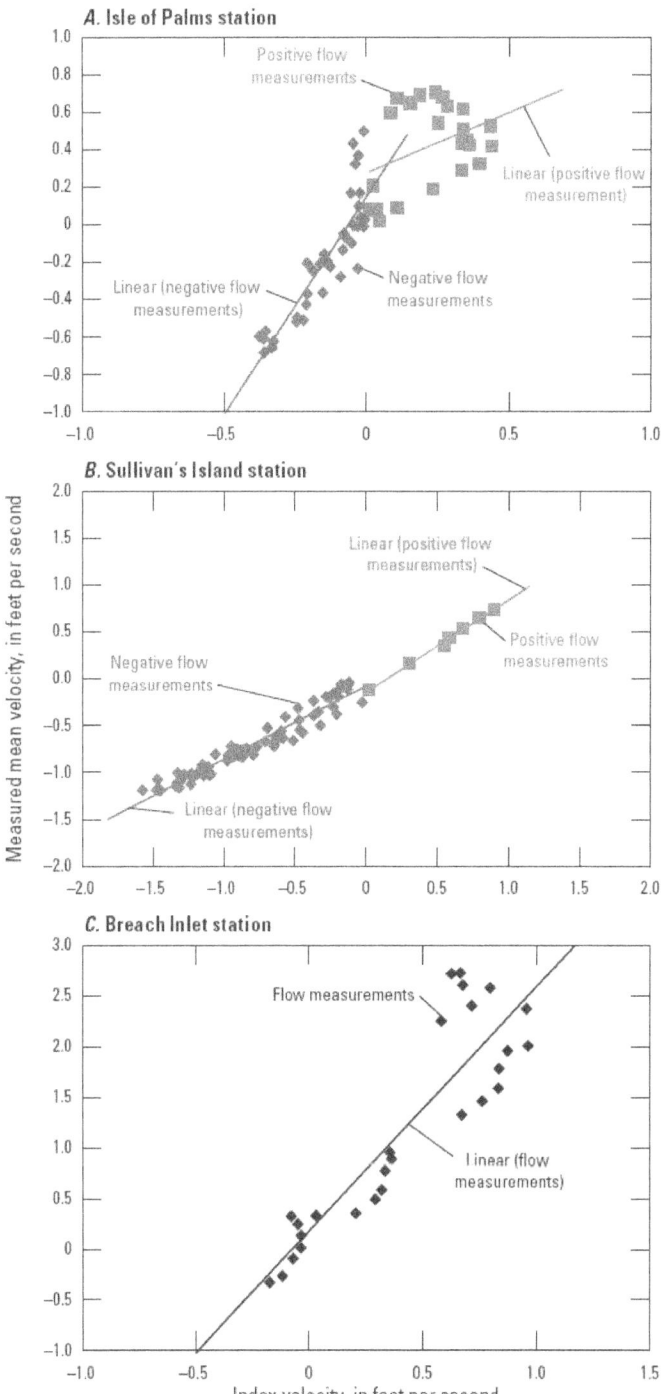

Figure 6. Index-velocity ratings for the A, Isle of Palms station, B, the Sullivan's Island station, and C, the Breach Inlet station.

Table 5.   Minimum, maximum, and average computed flows and residual flow for the period December 4, 2011, to January 26, 2012.

[ft³/s, cubic foot per second]

Station	Maximum negative flow (ft³/s)	Maximum positive flow (ft³/s)	Maximum residual negative flow (ft³/s)	Maximum residual positive flow (ft³/s)	Average residual flow (ft³/s)
Isle of Palms[1]	-3,460	6,410	-814	2,010	616
Sullivan's Island[1]	-6,360	8,930	-3,020	1,040	-866
Breach Inlet[2]	-58,600	63,300	-24,600	11,300	-5,770

[1]Positive flow is toward the northest and negative flow is toward the southwest.

[2]Positive flow is toward the Atlantic Ocean and negative flow is toward the Atlantic Intracoastal Waterway.

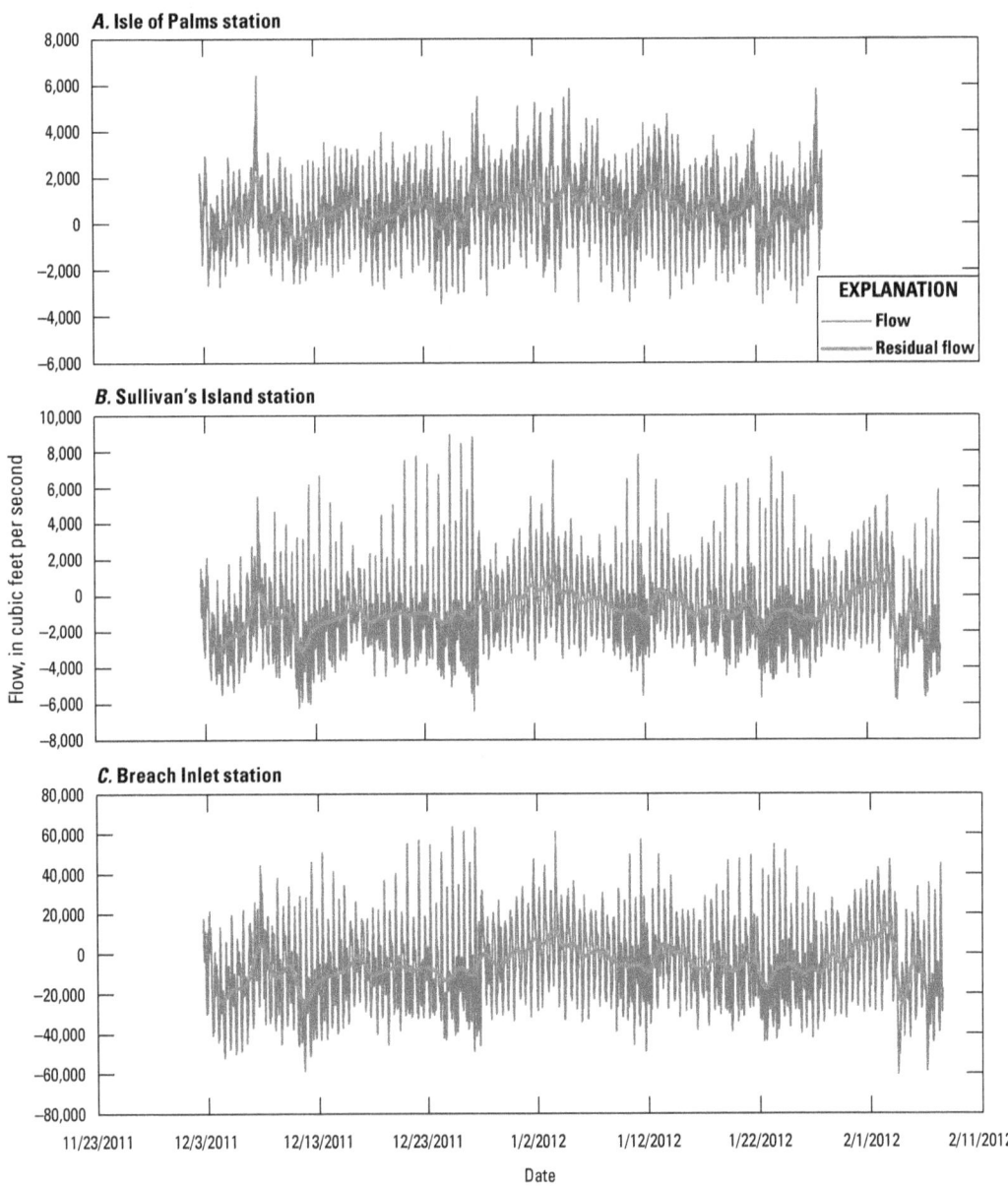

Figure 7.   Flow and residual flow for the *A*, Isle of Palms station, *B*, the Sullivan's Island station, and *C*, the Breach Inlet station.

-58,600 ft³/s to 63,300 ft³/s. The magnitude of flows at the IOP station ranged from -3,460 ft³/s to the southwest to 6,410 ft³/s to the northeast. At the SI station, the flows ranged from -6,360 to 8,930 ft³/s.

The residual flow directions and magnitudes were determined by using a low-pass filter to remove the semi-diurnal tidal signals from the 15-minute instantaneous computed flow data (Roberts and Roberts, 1978; Mathworks, 1998). Residual flow hydrographs for the IOP, SI, and BI stations are shown in figures 7 and 8. The differences in the magnitude and direction of the residual flow at the three stations is evident in figure 8. The average residual flows for the study period are 616 ft³/s to the northeast at the IOP station, -866 ft³/s to the southwest at the SI station, and -5,770 ft³/s into the Atlantic Intracoastal Waterway for the BI station (table 5).

The specific conductance at the IOP and SI stations are shown with the respective residual flow in figure 9. The specific conductance appears to be negatively correlated with the residual flow direction (generally northeast or southwest). Specific conductance generally decreases when residual flow to the northeast increases. To determine the hydraulic interaction between Charleston Harbor and the Atlantic Intracoastal Waterway, the specific conductance for the SI, IOP, and Cooper River at the Custom House (CH) stations were smoothed using a low-pass filter of nested 13- and 25-hour moving window averages and plotted along with the residual flows at the SI station (fig. 10). The lower specific-conductance water of Charleston Harbor and the decrease in specific conductance at the SI and IOP stations during periods of positive flow in the Atlantic Intracoastal Waterway may indicate the transport of lower specific-conductance water from Charleston Harbor to the northeast into the Atlantic Intracoastal Waterway during periods of positive flows to the northeast.

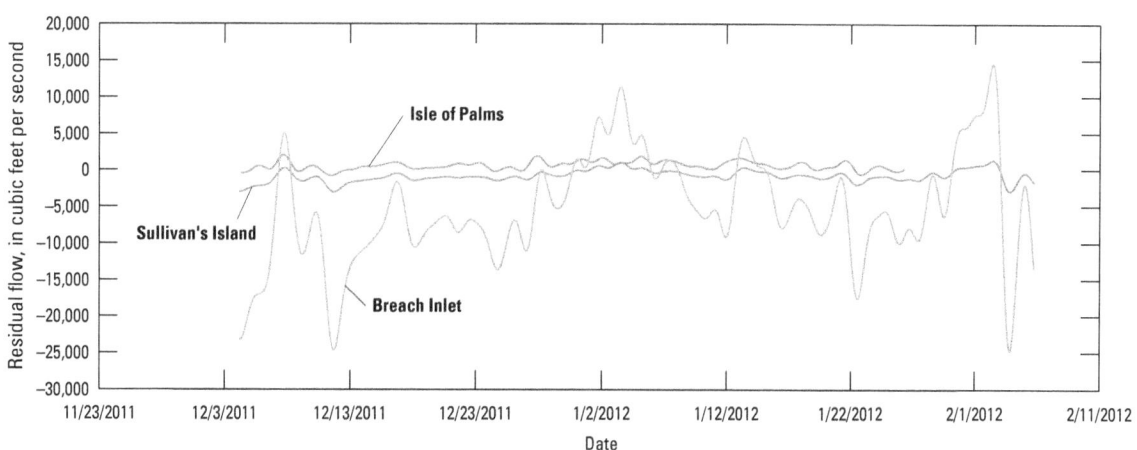

Figure 8. Residual flow for the Isle of Palms, the Sullivan's Island, and the Breach Inlet stations.

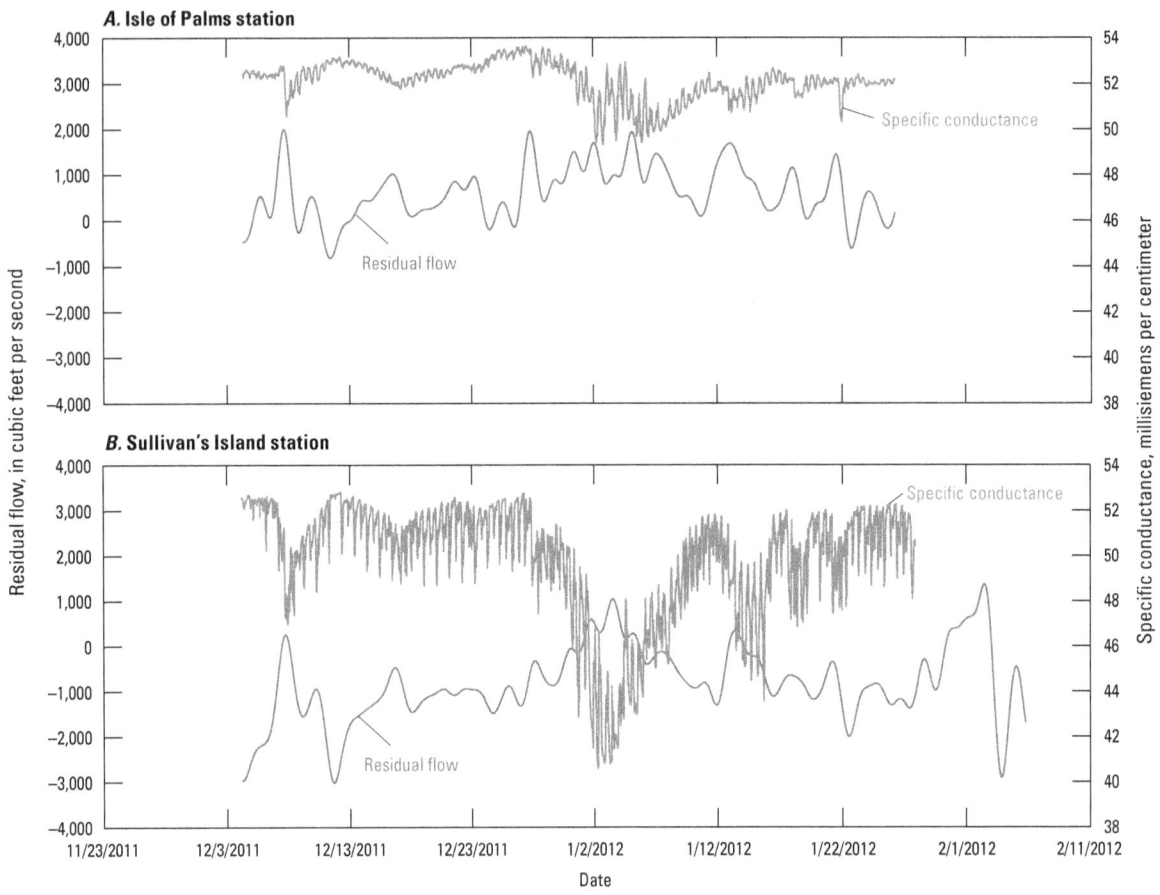

Figure 9.   Specific conductance and residual flow at the *A*, Isle of Palms and *B*, Sullivan's Island stations.

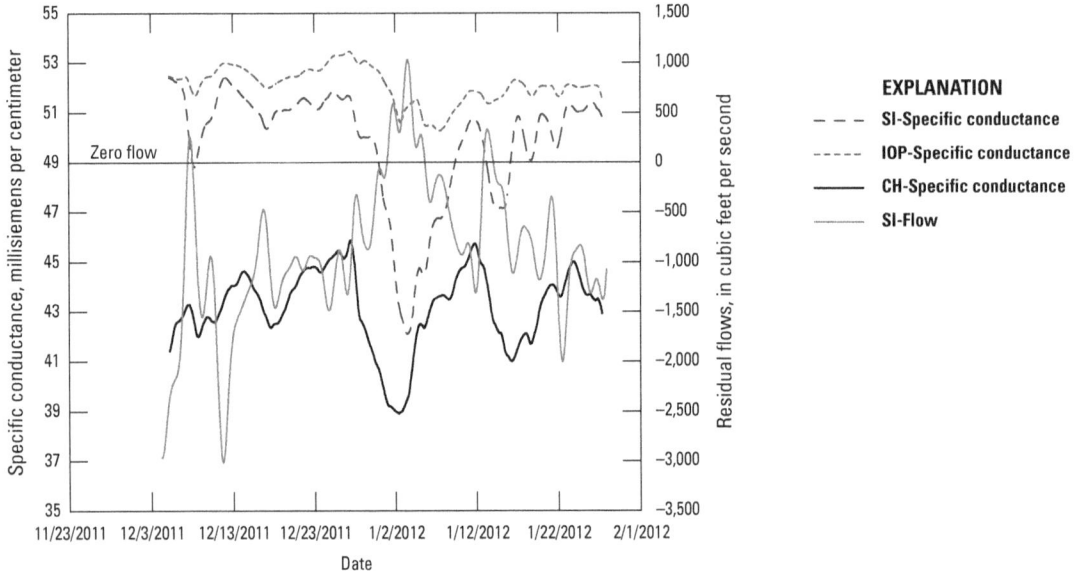

Figure 10.   Low-pass filtered specific conductance for Charleston Harbor (CH), Sullivan's Island (SI), and Isle of Palms and residual flows for Sullivan's Island (SI).

Assessment of Water-Quality and Background Fluorescence

Depth, water temperature, specific conductance, dissolved oxygen, pH, and fluorescence were summarized using statistical techniques. Water temperature, specific conductance, dissolved oxygen, and pH were comparable between the primary and secondary sonde, having a maximum variability at a site was 1.8 percent. Individually, the average variability between sondes of water temperature and specific conductance measurements was about 0.3 percent. The average variability of pH measurements between sondes was only 0.1 percent. Dissolved oxygen measurements displayed the greatest variability between sondes and had an average variability of 1.5 percent.

Measurements of background fluorescence in rhodamine concentrations and specific conductance at the selected stations were used as input into the established GIS point coverage. The inverse distance weighted (IDW) interpolation technique using ArcGIS Spatial Analyst (ESRI, 2011) was applied to the data to interpolate values between the measured locations and produce a surface layer of the data that represented the study area. The IDW interpolation implements the assumption that things closer to one another are more alike than those farther apart (ESRI, 2011). Therefore, sampled points closest to areas of interpolation will exert more influence on the interpolation than sampled points farther way.

Basic Water Chemistry at Profile Stations

During high-tide and low-tide conditions, water-quality measurements were collected at selected locations in the study area (table 6-7, fig. 1). During high-tide conditions, water temperatures ranged from 12.2 to 14.4 °C and had a median of 12.5 °C at all stations and all depths (table 6). Maximum water temperatures were measured during ebb tide at station 18, located on Hamlin Creek north of the Atlantic Intracoastal Waterway in the Isle of Palms (table 7). Specific conductance ranged from 49.2 to 53.1 millisiemens per centimeter (mS/cm) and had a median of 52.9 mS/cm. Dissolved oxygen concentrations ranged from 7.6 to 8.5 milligrams per liter (mg/L) and had a median of 8.3 mg/L. For the water temperature and barometric pressure conditions (764 millimeters of mercury) at the time of sampling, the dissolved oxygen concentrations measured at the stations in the Atlantic Intracoastal Waterway represented about 75-percent saturation during high-tide conditions. Measurements of pH were relatively stable among profile stations and depths, ranging from 7.8 to 8.0.

At the 3 transects (stations 12, 14, and 17) where 3 points were measured during high tide (table 7), horizontal (bank-to-bank) variability along the profile transect was less than 1.2 percent for water temperature, specific conductance, dissolved oxygen, and pH, indicating well-mixed conditions. In general, water temperature varied between 0 and 0.1 °C; specific conductance varied between 0 and 100 mS/cm (0 to 0.2 percent of reading); dissolved oxygen varied between 0 and 0.1 mg/L; and pH varied less than 0.1 standard units.

Table 6.   Descriptive statistical summary of the water-quality measurements collected at selected sites in the Atlantic Intracoastal Waterway near Sullivan's Island and Isle of Palms, South Carolina, on January 24, 2012.

[ft, foot; C, degrees Celsius; mS/cm, millisiemens per centimeter at 25 degrees Celsius; mg/L, milligrams per liter; μg/L, micrograms per liter]

Statistic	Depth (ft)	Water temperature (°C)	Specific conductance (mS/cm)	Dissolved oxygen (mg/L)	pH (units)	Fluorescence, field (μg/L)
High-tide conditions						
Minimum	1.0	12.2	49.2	7.6	7.8	0.0
1st Quartile	1.0	12.3	52.7	8.1	8.0	0.2
Mean	4.9	12.6	52.4	8.2	8.0	0.3
Median	5.0	12.5	52.9	8.3	8.0	0.3
3rd Quartile	5.0	12.8	53.0	8.4	8.0	0.4
Maximum	15.0	14.4	53.1	8.5	8.0	0.7
Low-tide conditions						
Minimum	1.0	12.7	48.4	7.8	7.9	0.0
1st Quartile	1.0	13.5	50.8	7.8	7.9	0.1
Mean	4.2	13.7	51.8	8.1	7.9	0.2
Median	5.0	13.7	52.6	8.1	7.9	0.2
3rd Quartile	5.0	13.8	52.7	8.2	7.9	0.2
Maximum	10.0	15.0	52.9	8.5	8.0	0.5

Table 7. Water-quality measurements collected at selected points along the cross section in the channel during high-tide conditions at selected sites in the Atlantic Intracoastal Waterway near Sullivan's Island and Isle of Palms, South Carolina, on January 24, 2012.

[RB, right bank; US, upstream; NE, northeast; %, percent; ft, foot; C, degrees Celsius; mS/cm, millisiemens per centimeter at 25 degrees Celsius; mg/L, milligrams per liter; µg/L, micrograms per liter; AIW, Atlantic Intracoastal Waterway; WWTP, wastewater treatment plant; S.C., South Carolina; ND, not determined]

Station number (fig. 1)	Station description	Cross section location from RB looking US/NE (%)	Time	Depth (ft)	Water temperature (°C)	Specific conductance (mS/cm)	Dissolved oxygen (mg/L)	pH (units)	Fluorescence, field (µg/L)
2	AIW at mouth of The Cove near Sullivan's Island	50	1035	1	12.8	49.2	8.5	8.0	0.2
			1036	5	12.6	49.9	8.4	8.0	0.3
			1037	10	12.5	50.6	8.3	8.0	0.4
3	Unnamed cove off AIW at the WWTP outfall in Sullivan's Island	50	1030	1	13.1	49.9	8.0	7.9	0.3
			1031	3	13.1	50.1	7.9	7.9	0.5
4	AIW at the east side of S.C. Highway 703 (Ben Sawyer) Bridge in Sullivan's Island	50	1023	1	12.7	49.3	8.4	8.0	0.3
			1024	5	12.5	50.2	8.3	8.0	0.3
			1025	10	12.6	51.1	8.2	8.0	0.0
			1026	15	12.7	52.6	7.9	7.9	0.6
6	West fork of Conch Creek nr Sullivan's Island within shellfish harvesting area	50	1052	1	13.1	52.9	8.0	8.0	0.3
			1053	5	13.1	52.9	8.0	8.0	0.3
			1054	10	13.1	52.9	8.0	8.0	0.1
7	East Fork of Conch Creek near Sullivan's Island within shellfish harvesting area	50	1100	1	12.9	52.9	8.1	8.0	0.4
			1101	5	12.9	52.9	8.0	8.0	0.1
			1102	10	12.9	52.9	8.0	8.0	0.1
9	AIW before the mouth of Inlet Creek near Sullivan's Island	50	1009	1	12.6	51.7	8.3	8.0	0.2
			1010	5	12.6	51.8	8.2	8.0	0.2
			1011	10	12.5	51.9	8.2	8.0	0.2
12	AIW before the mouth of Swinton Creek near Isle of Palms	50	0826	1	12.2	52.6	8.5	8.0	0.5
			0827	5	12.2	52.7	8.5	8.0	0.3
			0830	10	12.2	53.0	8.5	8.0	0.3
12	AIW before the mouth of Swinton Creek near Isle of Palms	25	0835	1	12.2	53.1	8.5	8.0	0.3
			0837	5	12.2	53.1	8.5	8.0	0.2
12	AIW before the mouth of Swinton Creek near Isle of Palms	75	0840	1	12.3	53.1	8.4	8.0	0.7
			0841	5	12.3	53.1	8.4	8.0	0.4
13	AIW at the Isle of Palms connector bridge at Isle of Palms	50	0845	1	12.2	52.9	8.4	8.0	0.2
			0850	5	12.2	53.0	8.4	8.0	0.6
			0851	10	12.2	53.0	8.4	8.0	0.3

Table 7. Water-quality measurements collected at selected points along the cross section in the channel during high-tide conditions at selected sites in the Atlantic Intracoastal Waterway near Sullivan's Island and Isle of Palms, South Carolina, on January 24, 2012.—Continued

[RB, right bank; US, upstream; NE, northeast; %, percent; ft, foot; C, degrees Celsius; mS/cm, millisiemens per centimeter at 25 degrees Celsius; mg/L, milligrams per liter; μg/L, micrograms per liter; AIW, Atlantic Intracoastal Waterway; WWTP, wastewater treatment plant; S.C., South Carolina; ND, not determined]

Station number (fig. 1)	Station description	Cross section location from RB looking US/NE (%)	Time	Depth (ft)	Water temperature (°C)	Specific conductance (mS/cm)	Dissolved oxygen (mg/L)	pH (units)	Fluorescence, field (μg/L)
14	Hamlin Creek near its mouth near Goat Island at Isle of Palms in shellfish harvesting areas	25	0911	1	12.4	52.8	8.3	8.0	0.2
			0912	5	12.4	52.9	8.3	8.0	0.2
14	Hamlin Creek near its mouth near Goat Island at Isle of Palms in shellfish harvesting areas	50	0914	1	12.3	52.9	8.4	8.0	0.4
			0915	5	12.3	53.0	8.4	8.0	0.6
			0916	10	12.3	53.0	8.4	8.0	0.5
14	Hamlin Creek near its mouth near Goat Island at Isle of Palms in shellfish harvesting areas	75	0917	1	12.4	53.0	8.3	8.0	0.1
			0918	5	12.4	53.0	8.3	8.0	0.3
15	AIW at Goat Island	50	0925	1	12.8	52.9	8.1	8.0	0.2
			0926	5	12.7	52.9	8.2	8.0	0.3
			0927	10	12.5	53.0	8.2	8.0	0.5
16	AIW at Isle of Palms Marina index-velocity station	50	0935	1	13.1	52.8	8.0	7.9	0.2
			0936	5	13.0	52.8	7.9	7.9	0.4
			0937	10	13.0	52.8	7.9	7.9	0.1
			0938	15	12.8	52.9	7.8	7.9	0.0
17	AIW at the Isle of Palms WWTP outfall east of Isle of Palms Connector Bridge	25	0859	1	12.4	53.0	8.4	8.0	0.3
			0900	5	ND	ND	ND	ND	0.3
17	AIW at the Isle of Palms WWTP outfall east of Isle of Palms Connector Bridge	50	0901	1	12.4	53.0	8.3	8.0	0.2
			0902	5	12.4	53.0	8.3	8.0	0.3
			0903	10	12.3	53.0	8.3	8.0	0.4
17	AIW at the Isle of Palms WWTP outfall east of Isle of Palms Connector Bridge	75	0905	1	12.3	52.9	8.4	8.0	0.6
			0906	5	12.3	53.0	8.4	8.0	0.6
18	Hamlin Creek north of AIW in Isle of Palms	50	1119	1	14.4	52.7	7.6	7.8	0.4
			1120	5	14.3	52.8	7.6	7.8	0.3
21	Hamlin Creek south of AIW in Isle of Palms	50	0953	1	12.4	53.0	8.4	8.0	0.3
			0954	5	12.3	53.1	8.4	8.0	0.6
			0956	10	12.3	53.1	8.4	8.0	0.4
21	Hamlin Creek south of AIW in Isle of Palms	75	1000	1	12.5	53.0	8.3	8.0	0.3
			1002	10	12.4	53.0	8.3	8.0	0.2

During low-tide conditions, water temperatures collectively ranged from 12.7 to 15.0 °C and had a median value of 13.7 °C for all stations and all depths (tables 6 and 8). Maximum water temperatures were measured at station 3, located in an unnamed cove off the Atlantic Intracoastal Waterway near the wastewater treatment plant outfall in Sullivan's Island (table 8). Specific conductance ranged from 48.4 to 52.9 mS/cm and had a median of 52.6 mS/cm. Dissolved oxygen concentrations ranged from 7.8 to 8.5 mg/L and had a median of 8.1 mg/L. For the water temperature and barometric pressure conditions (764 millimeters of mercury) at the time of sampling, the dissolved oxygen concentrations measured at the stations in the Atlantic Intracoastal Waterway also represented about 75-percent saturation during low-tide conditions. Measurements of pH were relatively stable among profile stations and depths, ranging from 7.9 to 8.0.

Stations were well mixed vertically, with water temperature, specific conductance, dissolved oxygen, and pH, varying minimally with depth (table 8). The percent variability in water temperature with depth ranged from -2.6 to 0.1 percent from the water surface to channel bottom during high-tide conditions and from -7.2 to -0.2 percent during low-tide conditions. A negative percentage indicated a decreasing trend from surface to bottom, whereas a positive percentage indicated increasing trend from surface to bottom. The variation in specific conductance with depth (from surface to bottom) ranged from 0 to 6.2 percent during high-tide conditions and from 0 to 4.2 percent during low-tide conditions. Dissolved oxygen measurements varied from -6.1 to 0.9 percent from surface to bottom during high-tide conditions and from -5.2 to 0.1 percent during low-tide conditions. Measurements of pH were the least variable with depth, ranging from -0.8 to 0.4 percent during high-tide conditions and from -0.6 to 0.4 percent during low-tide conditions.

Background Fluorescence and Specific Conductance

Background fluorescence (recorded as rhodamine) concentrations were all below 1 microgram per liter (µg/L), which is the accuracy level of the sensor (table 3), so measurements should be compared with caution. Additionally, fluorescence varied vertically and horizontally, whereby small differences in magnitude produced large differences in percentages. Therefore, differences in mixing for fluorescence were expressed in micrograms per liter of rhodamine, rather than in percent. In general, horizontal variability at the profile transects at stations 12, 14, and 17 and vertical (depth) variability in fluorescence ranged from 0.1 to 0.4 µg/L. Ranges of horizontal and vertical variability at individual stations were similar to ranges of spatial (among station) variability, increasing the uncertainty when comparing stations.

During high-tide conditions, an apparent pattern of slightly elevated fluorescence (near 0.5 and 0.6 µg/L) in specific regions of the Atlantic Intracoastal Waterway and nearby coves and tidal creeks was observed in the IDW distribution map (fig. 11). These regions included Hamlin Creek, the Atlantic Intracoastal Waterway near the mouth of Hamlin Creek (stations 14, 18, and 21), especially at the greater (5 ft and 10 ft) depths (fig. 11C,E. Fluorescence appeared to be higher at near-surface (1-ft) depths than greater depths (5 ft and 10-ft) during high tide in Conch Creek (fig. 11A,C,F) (stations 6 and 7) and highest at greater-depth (10 ft) during high tide in Hamlin Creek (fig. 11A,C,F) (stations 14 and 18). The IDW interpolation of specific conductance, also mapped for high-tide conditions, indicated small increases in specific conductance from the southwest (Sullivan's Island) to northeast (Isle of Palms) in the Atlantic Intracoastal Waterway, and in Hamlin and Conch Creeks (fig. 11B,D,F). This spatial change in specific conductance was observed at all 3 depths in the water column.

A pattern of slightly elevated fluorescence was also observed during low-tide conditions in the region of Hamlin Creek and the Atlantic Intracoastal Waterway near the mouth of Hamlin Creek in the IDW distribution map (fig. 12A,C,E), but unlike the case during high-tide conditions, not in the other tidal creeks. Near the Ben M. Sawyer Memorial Bridge (State Highway 703) at Sullivan's Island, slightly higher fluorescence was observed at 1- and 5-ft depths (fig. 12A,C). Spatial distribution of specific conductance during low-tide conditions had a similar pattern of increasing specific conductance from southwest (Sullivan's Island) to northeast (Isle of Palms) in the Atlantic Intracoastal Waterway and (fig. 12B,D,F). Graphs showing fluorescence concentrations and specific conductance in the Atlantic Intracoastal Waterway and nearby tidal creeks on January 24, 2012, during low-tide conditions, Sullivan's Island and Isle of Palms, South Carolina.

Although areas within the Atlantic Intracoastal Waterway and tidal creeks appeared to have slightly elevated fluorescence, all measured concentrations were below the accuracy of the sensor. Therefore, the measured background fluorescence would be unlikely to interfere with a dye-tracing study, if sufficient dye were to be released to raise levels well above the accuracy level of 1 µg/L. Additionally, changes in water temperature, pH, and dissolved oxygen concentrations have been identified to affect dye fluorescence in ambient waters, and results from this study indicated a relatively well-mixed system in terms of those factors (YSI Incorporated, 2001, 2011). Low measured concentrations produced a large amount of uncertainty about whether the apparent slight elevation of the fluorescence was related to optical brighteners in wastewater effluent, turbidity (not measured during the study) interference with the fluorescence probe sensor, high naturally occurring organic compounds interference, or simply poor sensor performance at concentrations below its accuracy level.

Table 8. Water-quality measurements collected in the center of the channel during low-tide conditions at selected stations in the Atlantic Intracoastal Waterway near Sullivan's Island and Isle of Palms, South Carolina, on January 24, 2012.

[ft, foot; C, degrees Celsius; mS/cm, milliSiemens per centimeter at 25 degrees Celsius; mg/L, milligrams per liter; AIW, Atlantic Intracoastal Waterway; µg/L, micrograms per liter; AIW, Atlantic Intracoastal Waterway; WWTP, wastewater treatment plant; S.C., South Carolina]

Station number (fig. 1)	Station description	Time	Depth (ft)	Water temperature (°C)	Specific conductance (mS/cm)	Dissolved oxygen (mg/L)	pH (units)	Rhodamine, field (µg/L)
1	AIW in The Cove near Sullivan's Island	1415	1	14.3	48.4	8.1	7.9	0.3
		1416	5	13.7	50.0	8.2	7.9	0.2
		1418	10	13.4	50.5	8.1	7.9	0.2
2	AIW at mouth of The Cove near Sullivan's Island	1405	1	13.8	50.5	8.2	7.9	0.1
3	Unnamed cove off AIW at the WWTP outfall in Sullivan's Island	1400	1	15.0	50.8	8.3	7.9	0.2
4	AIW at the east side of S.C. Highway 703 (Ben Sawyer) Bridge in Sullivan's Island	1350	1	13.7	50.3	8.5	8.0	0.1
		1352	5	13.3	52.2	8.3	8.0	0.4
5	AIW between the mouths of Narrows and Conch Creeks near Sullivan's Island	1340	1	13.8	51.3	8.4	8.0	0.0
		1341	5	13.6	52.4	8.1	7.9	0.2
		1342	10	13.4	52.5	7.9	7.9	0.0
12	AIW before the mouth of Swinton Creek near Isle of Palms	1335	1	13.8	52.7	7.8	7.9	0.2
		1337	5	13.8	52.7	7.8	7.9	0.2
13	AIW at the Isle of Palms connector bridge at Isle of Palms	1327	1	13.9	52.7	7.8	7.9	0.2
		1330	5	13.8	52.8	7.8	7.9	0.3
16	AIW at the Isle of Palms Marina index-velocity station	1310	1	13.6	52.7	8.2	7.9	0.1
		1312	5	13.0	52.8	8.2	8.0	0.2
		1313	10	12.7	52.9	8.2	8.0	0.1
17	AIW at the Isle of Palms WWTP outfall east of Isle of Palms Connector Bridge	1320	1	13.7	52.7	7.8	7.9	0.2
		1321	5	13.6	52.8	7.8	7.9	0.5
		1322	10	13.6	52.8	7.8	7.9	0.5

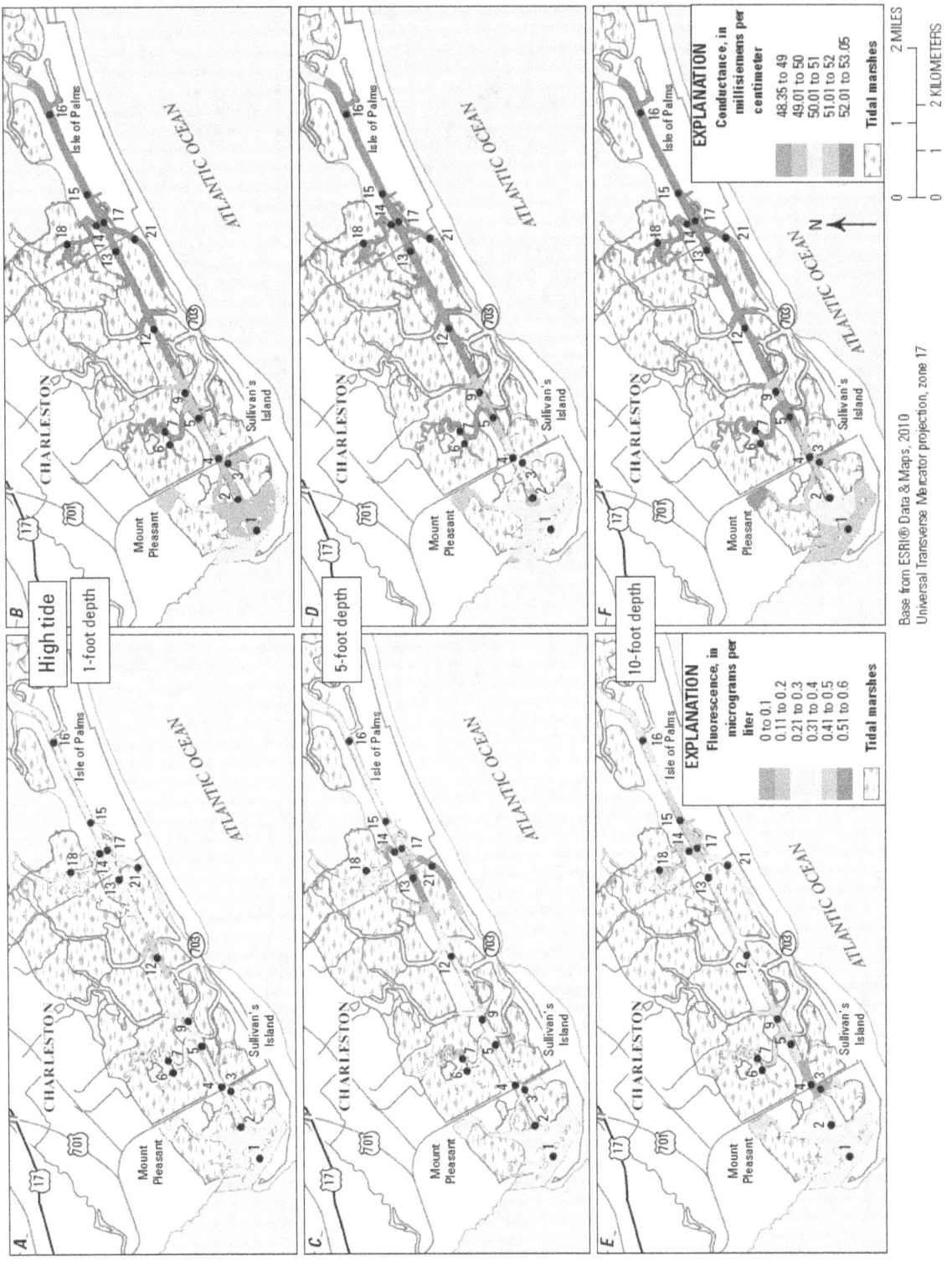

Figure 11. Fluorescence concentrations and specific conductance in the Atlantic Intracoastal Waterway and nearby tidal creeks on January 24, 2012, during high-tide conditions, Sullivan's Island and Isle of Palms, South Carolina.

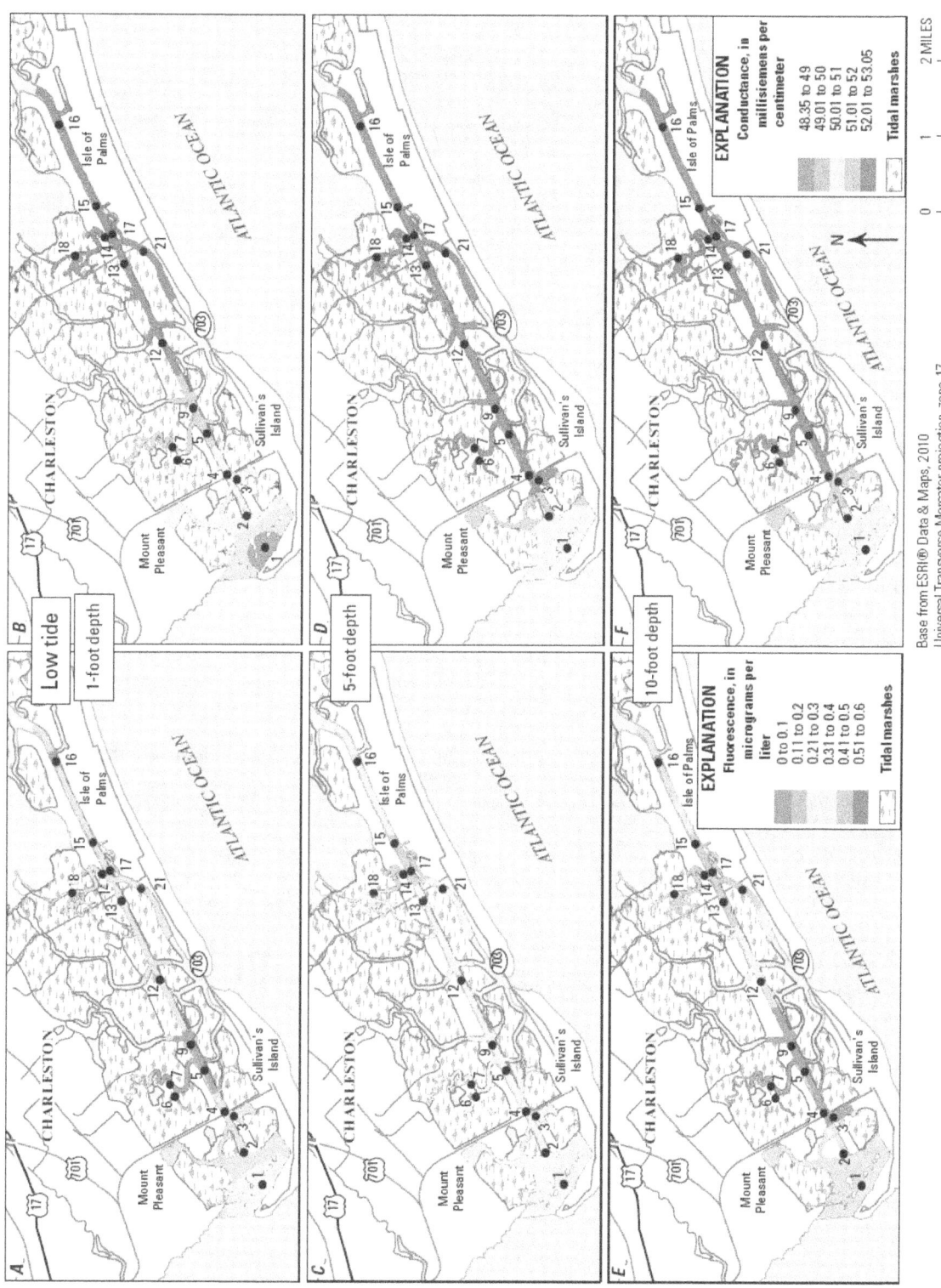

Figure 12. Fluorescence concentrations and specific conductance in the Atlantic Intracoastal Waterway and nearby tidal creeks on January 24, 2012, during low-tide conditions, Sullivan's Island and Isle of Palms, South Carolina.

Summary

Proposed changes in the water-quality limits for fecal coliform may have potential effects on the shellfish beds near the effluent outfalls of the Sullivan's Island and the Isle of Palms wastewater treatment plants. To effectively plan a site specific study to understand the connection between wastewater effluent and the shellfish beds, data are needed on the flow dynamics and background fluorescence of the Atlantic Intracoastal Waterway near the effluent outfalls on Sullivan's Island and the Isle of Palms. To compute continuous tidal flows, two index-velocity stations were installed and operated on the Atlantic Intracoastal Waterway at the Isle of Palms Marina and at the Ben M. Sawyer Memorial Bridge near Sullivan's Island. Tidal flows were estimated for Breach Inlet as a remote index-velocity station using the continuous 15-minute stage and velocity data from the Sullivan's Island station. To measure the background fluorescence of the Atlantic Intracoastal Waterway, a synoptic water-quality study was conducted to collect longitudinal water-quality profile locations along the Atlantic Intracoastal Waterway and included stations near the effluent receiving creeks, tidal creeks, and coves.

The two index-velocity stations measured concurrent data for the 53-day period of December 4, 2011, to January 26, 2012. Tidal flow and residual flow for the 53-day period on the Atlantic Intracoastal Waterway at the Isle of Palms stations ranged -3,460 cubic feet per second (ft^3/s) toward the southwest (toward Charleston Harbor) to 6,410 ft^3/s toward the northeast. For Sullivan's Island, the flows ranged from -6,360 ft^3/s to the southwest to 8,930 ft^3/s toward the northeast. The largest flows occurred at Breach Inlet and ranged from -58,600 ft^3/s toward the Atlantic Intracoastal Waterway and 63,300 ft^3/s toward the Atlantic Ocean. The residual flow during the 53-day period was -5,770 ft^3/s into the system toward the Atlantic Intracoastal Waterway at the Breach Inlet station. At the Isle of Palms station, the residual flow for the same period was 616 ft^3/s toward the northeast where it was -866 ft^3/s toward the southwest at the Sullivan's Island station.

Synoptic longitudinal water-quality profiles at high and low tide were sampled on January 24, 2012. Profile data included depth, water temperature, specific conductance, dissolved oxygen, pH, and background fluorescence. Generally, the stations were well mixed vertically and horizontally with respect to water temperature, pH, and dissolved oxygen. Maps of background fluorescence and specific conductance were generated for high- and low-tide and for 1-, 5-, and 10-foot depth using an inverse distance weighted interpolation technique. All the fluorescence measurements were below the accuracy of sensor. The background fluorescence would unlikely interfere with a dye-tracer study.

References Cited

ESRI, 2011, How IDW works: ArcGIS Help Library, accessed November 13, 2012, at *http://help.arcgis.com/en/arcgisdesktop/10.0/help/index.html#/How_IDW_works/009z00000075000000/*.

Hartel, P.G., Hagedorn, C., McDonald, J.L., Fisher, J.A., Saluta, M.A., Dickerson Jr., J.W., Gentit, L.C., Smith, S.L., Mantripragada, N.S., Ritter, K.J., and Belcher, C.N., 2007, Exposing water samples to ultraviolet light improves fluorometry for detecting human fecal contamination: Water Research, v. 41, p. 3629–3642.

Levesque, V.A., and Oberg, K.A., 2012, Computing discharge using the index velocity method: U.S. Geological Survey Techniques and Methods book 3, chap. A23, 148 p. (also available at *http://pubs.usgs.gov/tm/3a23/*).

Mathworks, 1998, Matlab Signal Processing Toolbox User's Guide: The Mathworks, Inc., chapter 6, p. 29, 34, 134.

Mueller, D.S., and Wagner, C.R., 2009, Measuring discharge with acoustic Doppler current profilers from a moving boat: U.S. Geological Survey Techniques and Methods book 3, chap. A22, 72 p. (also available at *http://pubs.water.usgs.gov/tm3a22*).

Roberts, Jo, and Roberts, T.D., 1978, Use of the Butterworth low-pass filter for oceanographic data: Journal of Geophysical Research, v. 83, no. C11, p. 5510–5514.

SonTek, 2009, Argonaut™-SL System Manual Firmware Version 12.0: San Diego, Calif., SonTek™/YSI Corporation, 316 p.

Teledyne RD Instruments, 2008, Workhorse Rio Grande ADCP: Accessed December 15, 2008, at *http://www.rdinstruments.com/datasheets/rio_grande_ds_lr.pdf*.

Wilde, F.D., ed., variously dated, Field measurements: U.S. Geological Survey Techniques of Water-Resources Investigations, book 9, chap. A6, with sec. 6.0–6.8, accessed March 15, 2012, at *http://pubs.water.usgs.gov/twri9A6/*.

YSI Incorporated, 2001, Water tracing, *in situ* dye fluorometry, and the YSI 6130 Rhodamine WT Sensor: YSI Environmental White Paper, accessed November 9, 2012, at *http://www.ysi.com/media/pdfs/E46-01_Rhodamine_Paper.pdf*.

YSI Incorporated, 2011, 6-Series multiparameter water quality sondes user manual: YSI Incorporated, accessed March 15, 2012, at *http://www.ysi.com/media/pdfs/069300-YSI-6-Series-Manual-RevH.pdf*.

www.ingramcontent.com/pod-product-compliance
Lightning Source LLC
Chambersburg PA
CBHW080359290526
45791CB00009BA/2925